The Unemployed Man Who Became A Tree

The Unemployed Man
Who Became A Tree

poems

Kevin Pilkington

Black Lawrence Press
www.blacklawrence.com

Executive Editor: Diane Goettel
Book Design: Steven Seighman

Text copyright © 2011 Kevin Pilkington

All rights reserved. Except for brief quotations in critical articles or reviews, no part of this book may be reproduced in any manner without prior written permission from the publisher:

Black Lawrence Press
115 Center Ave
Aspinwall, PA 15215
U.S.A.

Published 2011 by Black Lawrence Press, an imprint of Dzanc Books

ISBN: 978-09826364-6-6

First edition 2011

Printed in the United States

Contents

I. Street Music

- 13   Insomnia
- 15   Milk
- 16   Looking for Work
- 18   The Corner
- 20   Promises
- 21   The Distance Between Fog and Times Square
- 22   Peter Pan Listens to Sarah Vaughan
- 23   Walking Across America
- 25   On Cold Days Like This
- 26   The Week the Factory and Pancreas Closed Down
- 27   Travel
- 28   The Unemployed Man Who Became A Tree
- 29   Antigua
- 31   On Time for Miracles
- 33   It's About Time
- 35   Street Music

II. Parthenon

- 39   Santorini
- 41   Santorini at Night
- 42   Postcard
- 43   Greek Wedding
- 44   Like the Aegean
- 46   Athens
- 48   Parthenon

III. The View from Here

- 53   Marriage Advice
- 55   3:00AM
- 57   The Cape
- 59   Key West
- 61   My Mother's Clothes
- 63   Exercise
- 65   White Curtain
- 67   Boys Can't Be Trusted
- 69   Scattered Crumbs
- 71   Donuts
- 72   The Cat That Could Fly
- 73   Anniversary
- 75   Sunset in the Refrigerator
- 76   The Reincarnation of Bagels
- 78   Lucky Man
- 80   Afterlife
- 82   The View from Here

Once again, for Celia

"Anything for the quiet life."
           Seamus Heaney

"You few who understand know when death is
near the food you give your soul must be supreme."
           Semonides

"Time will not be ours forever;
He at length our good will sever.
Spend not then his gifts in vain,
Suns that set may rise again."
           Ben Johnson

I. Street Music

Insomnia

You can never see the moon
that should be hanging over
Fourth Street and since you know
all about compromise you settle
for yellow circles from traffic
lights that slide across
the bedroom wall.

Most nights are like this—
not being able to sleep.
If you doze it's usually too
late to dream so you sweat
and don't even bother to turn
on the fan since like everything
else lately, it only blows.

When the walls begin to talk
or mumble it's usually a tv
in the next apartment and
for some reason you are back
in your parents' living room
watching their old black and white
RCA, everyone on the screen
the color of priests and nuns.

Your mother is on the couch,
her belly big as a basketball
filled with your sister. And now
your sister with kids
of her own and a son who
is already the age of a good
bottle of scotch. You love him,
he loves the Knicks, but what matters
most is his sweet outside shot.

Every woman you ever dated
must have all gotten together
and taken the early morning express
bus into the city. There's no other
way to explain the chill
in the breeze that just came
through the window.

And when you hear a cop car
hit some potholes then watch
its red light, the color of the sore
throat you just got rid of, speed
across the ceiling, it makes you
realize how lonely you are.
As the siren fades you almost
wish it would come back, loud
enough this time so you could turn over
on your side, put your arm
around it and fall asleep.

Milk

On a warm night in upstate
New York during the summer
of 1948, Charlie Parker got out
of a brand new Pontiac, the bass
player from his quintet was behind
the wheel. Clubs along 57th Street
were an hour behind them. Parker
had grabbed the case with his sax
in it from the back seat and walked
out onto a field. He was off drugs,
clean for at least six months
but knew he'd never be clean
as the air he breathed.

A herd of cows watched him walk
in front of them, place the case
on the grass, open it and take out
a bent piece of sky the color of dawn.
Then he blew on it as his fingers
like a flock of small dark birds flew
up and down. The cows listened, stopped
chewing but couldn't prevent their tails
from swinging like the Basie rhythm
section. Sounds they never heard
came out of a hole in the sky.
Then it stopped. He placed it back
in the box and walked away. Within
hours the green grass they began
chewing again turned the milk in
their bellies white.

Looking for Work

I'd been out of work for a month
and knew it was time to get going
on my job search. So I got out
of bed, gazed out the window, looked
for a job, saw nothing that interested
me, crawled under the covers again
and fell back to sleep.

An hour later, I got up, brewed
coffee, made it strong, the color
of wet road, then traveled a mile
with my throat until the pot was empty.

I didn't go out at all the day
before but knew everything worth
missing was just outside my door
in the paper. Even with Monday
folded over with a crease through
noon, fifty cents seemed too
expensive for a day I basically
slept through.

The lead story reported a man
was shot just a few blocks
away, and though I hate guns,
I rifled through the rest of the paper,
tossed it on the floor then went
over to the refrigerator, even though
I don't believe in miracles and opened
it. None was going to take place on
that day either: no food appeared
just an old piece of steak I cooked once,
that looked raw as last December.

With the temperature reaching
for 90° again and knowing
it shouldn't reach for anything
beyond its grasp, I decided to get
dressed and walk over to St. James.
It's a Catholic church but since
the saints inside are still concrete,
I like to go in on weekdays where
it's cool, dark and empty. The strange
part is it feels like home. I've decided
it's the candles who look like my
relatives. Irish. Each flame a jig,
lit up on Guinness instead of matches.

The Corner

I stand on the corner
in the middle of a heat wave,
dressed in a white linen shirt
and pants with creases so sharp
I cut my finger putting them on.
It has been in the 90s all week
but it's clear to anyone who looks
my way where the coolest spot
in the city is today.

A red '56 Buick slides by
with the kind of curves
a man can only fantasize about
and makes any woman who looks
turn green. When a friend
of my father's walks by, stops
to say she heard he died
and was sorry for my loss,
there was no way to tell
her it was a profit, or running
every day for a month and
dropping ten pounds was
the real loss.

After she leaves, my brother
who lives around the block
walks by. We pretend
not to see each other since
we haven't spoken in over
a year. Even if I add a few
extra miles jogging, I'll never
be able to cover the distance
between us.

As I look over my shoulder
to see if he is gone, I catch
my reflection in the window
of the store I'm standing
in front of. Lights from the sign
above it and from the deli
next door melt across my face,
making me look like a Sioux
warrior on my way to Custer.
I like the look, then take
a cigar from my pocket, and
light it on the next hot breeze
that passes by, just to make sure
another hour will go up in smoke.

Promises

I'm standing at the corner
of Seventy-Second and York.
My niece who is eight and already
beautiful holds my hand. I warn
her again not to trust lights or cars
that fly by like summer.
She looks up and tells me not
to worry. She knows. But how
could she know I already worry
about the first guy who falls
in love with her. The kind of guy
who promises her the world, when
he can't even deliver Brooklyn.
Or the first guy she falls for, the one
who at night wants to take the lights
from buildings along Park and tie
them into a bracelet around her wrist
then slides the brightest light
from a penthouse on to her finger.
Before I can lean over to tell her
that the sparkle will go out as soon
as the sun comes up, she
points to the walk sign and says
we can go. Instead I remind her
to make sure the traffic light is red
and strong enough to stop
all the cars it should. As we
cross, a woman passes us
with a dog the color of smog.
My niece asks if I can get her
a puppy just like it. She's not allowed
to have pets yet but I find myself
promising to buy her a dog
that's even bigger, smarter
and with extra fur,
if she wants.

The Distance Between Fog and Times Square

After I moved into my first
apartment, every time the phone
rang I expected it to be
the voice of a woman sounding
like slow approaching fog
or a thousand Playboy
magazines. For months
I slept alone under an old
skylight on the top floor
of a five flight walk up.
Every time it stormed
raindrops hitting the glass
sounded like a typewriter
working on another story
until there was a sixth floor.
I soon learned what was real
in the city and what was fake.
The ten-inch statue in a shop
window along Times Square
could never be the Statue of Liberty
but did turn out to be the next woman
holding up her arm to hail a cab.

Peter Pan Listens
to Sarah Vaughn

You realize the woman you just
broke up with was too young
when she thought the fortieth
anniversary of the moonwalk
was about Michael Jackson.
You tried to make it work. After all
you'd like to see Neil Armstrong
try to cross the intersection on
Seventy-Second Street which would
make walking on the moon look easy.
You ended up blaming the Beatles
like you always do who broke up
too soon when you were a kid
and set a bad example you can't
seem to get over.

Things are changing which explains
how your niece who was four last
year is turning sixteen next week.
Every year there is another war
and now terrorism means not dancing fast
enough. Besides, you can always
turn your back on pigeons that sit
on the window sill like nuns praying
and feel no guilt whatsoever. Then
go over and start a fire in the fireplace
with your dog sleeping like a black and white
rug next to your chair, close your eyes
and listen to the fire as it burns
slowly and sings to you like Sarah Vaughan.

Walking Across America

Our third grade teacher
was a Dominican nun
who dressed in white robes.
Sister was short and thick
and when she stood still
to begin each day with a prayer
she looked like vanilla ice cream,
three scoops piled on top of each
other. Her black veil, chocolate
syrup pouring over her head
and down her back. I closed
my eyes and prayed for dessert.

The classroom was decorated
with letters of the alphabet, some
that for the last three years hadn't
made much sense. The C was an O
with its right side missing,
W was an M that fell on its head
and Z proved Zorro was still alive.

Math made even less sense –
the day three times two equaled
eight, the thick piece of plywood
that slammed against my back
was the palm of Sister's open hand.
And when she stood next to my desk
and shouted again, I closed
my eyes and braced myself. Six
was the lucky number that made
her move onto the kid at the desk
in front of mine.

During geography she told the class
to take out our large maps
of the US and spread them
across our desks. After I got
my pencil out, I noticed a tiny
roach standing on Maine.
It headed down along the East coast,
couldn't find Florida hanging over
the edge then headed west before
resting in Texas.

I kept watching as it made
its way to California and didn't
notice Sister walk by or her fist
shaped like a sledgehammer
come down and smash it all over
San Diego. She didn't even stop –
just kept walking up the aisle slowly,
the long rosary that hung on
to her belt rattling at her side.

On Cold Days Like This

I hear a cape flapping over
my head, convinced this time
it's Superman. When I look up
to greet him, it turns out to be
the flag over the doors of the Second
Avenue Post Office. The wind
is so strong I notice it lost a star
and wonder if maybe Utah is now
floating over New Jersey.

The traffic is heavy as cheesecake
and sounds like the Basie horn
section tuning up before a gig.
A guy walks over with a cigarette
in his mouth and asks if I got
a light. As I search my pockets
I notice his boots and cowboy
hat and figure he must be from
the west side. I can't find any—
consider the torch I'd been carrying
around for my ex but remember I put
it out a few days ago, tell him sorry.

And she was the same woman
who told me if we ever broke up
I'd be lost without her. Before
I got involved again, I made sure
to know every section of the city
until I knew it like the back
of my hand or when most of Second
Avenue ran down my index finger
towards my wrist. On cold days
like this, I can warm up my hands
and at least thirty blocks by simply
putting on my gloves.

The Week the Factory and Pancreas Closed Down

You were no more than eleven
waiting in the car in the A&P
parking lot while your mother
shopped and had to pee so badly
you got out and stood in front
of your dad's new Buick, leaned
up against it so no one could see,
opened your fly and started pissing.
You remember how you couldn't stop,
water draining out of you until
there was nothing left but sand
in your mouth and your eyes went
dry. You finally stopped when the grill
shaped like a smile frowned and all
you wanted to do was lie down like a lawn
and sleep. The factory right across
the street acted like your pancreas,
and went on strike the same week—one
stopped turning out ball bearings,
the other insulin. You considered
yourself luckier only ending up
with a loss of weight, a pitchfork of ribs
and diabetes—the factory with a loss
of jobs, boarded windows and rats.

Travel

I admit I see things a bit differently.
At the corner when the Don't Walk sign
lights up, its red hand stopping everyone
from crossing the street, I think it's an old
friend, so I wave, walk over to say hello
and almost get hit by a truck. And when
there is a sudden downpour, and everyone
starts to run trying not to get soaked, I
just tilt to the left, stroll between raindrops,
and stay perfectly dry. Then I stopped
looking at myself in storefront windows,
when I began to develop a crush, I'm
embarrassed to admit, on my reflection.
At least I knew enough to end things before
they went any further. For the past three
months though, I've been dating a woman
my friends make fun of whenever they see
us together. It's true she towers over me,
but I can't hear what they have to say since
I've never learned how to listen to anyone.
Besides, they never would understand how
I love to travel and at six feet, three inches
in heels, she is worth the trip.

The Unemployed Man Who Became a Tree

I lost my last job in July
then spent the rest of the summer
working on a tan. With little money
left, I searched the want ads
until coming across an opening
for a tree. The spot was just a few blocks
away near the path that runs along
the river. I hurried over to the square
patch of dirt in the concrete where
the city cut the last tree down.
Then stood on it, looked around,
liked the area and decided to take
the position. Within minutes my legs
went stiff as my feet began to root
the soil. My arms branched out,
skin became bark. The paper didn't
say what kind of tree was needed
although my limbs looked maple,
from the waist down, I was all oak.

By evening I was just about done
and even began thinking like wood:
how to bud April green enough
to get spring going early this year.
The only bird I ever cared about
was Charlie Parker, now I wanted
a flock to rest on my limbs,
build a nest on the highest branch
that sprouted from my ear –
a place to call home and a place safe
from cats. By evening the fog that crawled
in on its knees was gone and there I was,
alone, holding up the moon in my branch
shaped like a right hand for the entire
city to see – smiling.

Antigua

You are having a drink
in Redcliffe Quay.
Driving here you passed
goats that roam freely
on the island and noticed
one whose face looked like
Uncle Sam's under a tree
with palms shooting out
of its top like fireworks
on the Fourth of July. They
made you feel homesick
for the first time in weeks
and one more drink may help
you forget why you left.

At a table near you someone
is speaking German. Two
women speaking French
have drinks the color of sunset
and sip the sky through straws –
two guys at the bar are laughing
so loud anyone can translate it.
No one speaks English and if
you are honest with yourself,
you never really spoke it either.

The night sky here is warm
and black with a wide
smile and glittering jewels,
looking like the waitress
who brings you another local
drink with rum and a way
to go home. You decide to take
these languages, blend them

together into one, name it
after the next cool breeze, then
learn to speak it fluently.
When you are back in the States
and are rejected again and again
since no one understands
a word you are saying, at least
you will finally have the only
worthwhile reason for not ever
getting what you want.

On Time for Miracles

I'm fed up rooting for my
baseball team, turn down
the sound so they don't hear
me, then yell at the tv screen.
I wish I could bring
Benny Goodman to their next
practice so he could teach
them how to swing
and keep getting hits
for the next thirty years.

I look out the window
disgusted with how everything
is moving much too quickly
and keeps changing.
Summer is racing by again
and I consider bringing
what's left of it over
to the priest at St. Stevens
and ask him to put it
in his next sermon,
so the rest of August
will slow up and drag
on and on for a change.

A friend once told me
miracles happen every day.
I guess I never recognize
them or show up too late
the way I did when yogurt
became frozen. I made
a promise to myself to be there
for the next big one
like the loaves and fishes
or when spaghetti became pasta.

Just to make sure I won't
be late I always wear
a wristwatch now, and put
another in my back pocket
so even if I'm sitting down
I'll always be on time.

It's About Time
—for Maureen

Drinking coffee with my sister
in her kitchen, I give in and agree
being the only girl and the youngest
with three older brothers couldn't
have been easy. Try awful she adds
before taking another sip from her cup.
I knew my brothers and I teased her
so much she often cried but tried
to convince her we stopped when her
skin turned pink. And yes we did pinch
her on occasion, she was too cute not to.
The way she remembers, it was more
like every day. At least the hardest pinch
she still feels on her cheek came from
our oldest brother. That's why no one talks
to him anymore, I offer with a smile.
She just frowns, knows what I really mean
and asks if I want a refill.

As she pours more coffee into our cups,
I notice it has begun to flurry. It reminds
us again about how in our house as kids
snow was a four-letter word. It crippled
our dad's roofing company, his men couldn't
work and cost him a lot of money, he'd complain.
When school closed every storm and put
our dad in a bad mood, we couldn't show
how thrilled we were for the day off until
we went outside and played in drifts.
In summer we made sure to bring home
ice pops but never snow cones.

After our parents died, my sister made sure
my brothers and I who were still single
were invited to her house for dinners since we all
belonged together she told us. She was such
a great cook we always showed up often
at dinner time, on all major holidays,
then on holidays she never heard of.
After her son was born, I heard her say
on the phone she had one child, then looked
over at us finishing dessert and said,
but I have a lot of mouths to feed.

We both watch the snow falling and begin
to pile up like the pages in a new short
story she is working on. She complains about
not having enough time to write and asks
when will I finally write a poem about her.
I know she is only half kidding, though
she doesn't know this one is for her. So
I add the last two lines, leave out the stanza
about how lucky we are to be this close
for another poem, then slide it across
the table and ask her to read it. She puts on
her new glasses, that of course make her
look thinner, reads it, slowly takes them off
and says it's about time.

Street Music

I'm on the street
where a guy once walked
up next to me and asked
for my wallet. I looked
at him then down at
the knife he was holding
and the point he was
trying to make. I
was convinced and handed
it over. The year before
crime had come down
with the old tenements
and new buildings went
up faster than rents.
I watched him run across
town with what was left
of the old neighborhood
in his coat pocket.

The entire area is safer
now but more expensive.
The shops along Third
were torn down. Most
came back as French
or Italian boutiques, some
never came back or
were lost in the translation.
Across the street the tallest
building yet is under
construction; at the end
of the day workers come down
covered in white dust
from rubbing against clouds.
It's going up on the spot

where the magazine store
stood. Its owner ran it
for sixty years and had more
stories in him than the high-rise
ever will.

Some things in the area
aren't what they seem.
Two years ago the section
of the river that runs
along the north side started
to jog and its banks
filled with concrete slabs
now close on national holidays.
Although the traffic on First
is still heavy, cars
keep changing. What
stays the same and never
changes is the music
found in women walking
in heels that are so high
you need an elevator
just to reach their ankles.
Listen and you'll hear
their hips sway back
and forth with the kind
of songs you'll swallow
and never want to hum.

II. Parthenon

Santorini

I didn't know how high up
on the caldera our villa
was until I stood on the terrace
and looked down at a toy boat
a child lost, before realizing it was
a cruise ship and the yacht sailing
past Skaros, I could pick up
and put in my pocket along
with the rest of the Euro coins
I'd been carrying around since Athens.
And where the sun reached
the surface of the Aegean, candles
were flickering inside waves.

A woman standing on a rock
was the size of a matchstick
I thought about using to light
my cigar until I found my own,
lit up, then let smoke the size
of a cloud float out of my mouth,
since there was no rain in it
to spoil the day. And I've learned
the man yelling next door
is how Greeks whisper.

Tiny white churches no bigger
than doves are scattered all over
the island. A flock sits along
the cliffs leading towards the town
of Ia on the northern tip
of the caldera that from here looks
like vanilla icing melting over
a slice of rock.

I pull up a chair, sit down and
stare deeply into this view the way
I never could into the eyes of a woman
until they belonged to my wife,
let my skin turn the color
of iced tea, then noticed how there
were now white caps on the water,
or thousands of angels swimming
towards shore.

Santorini at Night

I sit on the terrace under
a moon that will stay Greek
until I leave. The sky is clear
and the air cool as Steve McQueen.
I can see Ia, a town on the northern tip
of the caldera, its lights glowing
like hot coals just perfect
for grilling steaks on. To the south,
the lighthouse on Akrotiri keeps
winking at me. I'm flattered
knowing the most beautiful
coastline I've ever seen
is hitting on me, but I can't
imagine acting on it or taking
the leap and dropping four
thousand feet—the only way to fall
in love with this view. And
there is the Big Dipper sparkling
like it belongs in my mother's
kitchen. A cruise ship moving
as slow as a Russian novel passes
under it and in front of an island
a volcano left for taking Atlantis.
It looks like a dog sleeping.
When I leave I plan to whistle
until it wakes, gets up, shakes
its rock into fur and follows me
all the way to the airport with its
tail wagging.

Postcard from Santorini

Friends:

Glad you aren't here. Our hotel is on the edge of a cliff, at least 6000 feet overlooking the Aegean. Wouldn't want to worry about any of you falling off. Atlantis is still under the water holding its breath; with my luck it will probably surface after I leave. The grilled octopus I've been eating every day looks like a special effect in a Spielberg movie. In fact, all the fish is fresh and caught the same day—not processed, frozen or sitting around for months the way we like it at home. All fast food here is slow and hundreds of small white churches are on the island, but lets face it God can't be in all of them at once. So I don't go to any, since I don't know which one he's staying in. If you are interested in the jewelry they sell here don't buy the diamond necklace that sparkles at night on the island across the way. It's a fake. In the morning when the sun comes up, you'll see it's a town you placed around your lover's neck. The ruins here are ancient towns and cities that look like your relationships and marriage but at least yours are recent. Those of you who no longer do coke or just got out of rehab might be tempted again watching cruise ships going in and out of port with long white lines in their wake. It's not what you think, but if you roll up a bill and stick it in your nose you'll just snort water. I don't want that on my conscience, so stay put. By the way, I won't be coming home at the end of the week like I planned.
Will write again soon,
    Kevin

Greek Wedding
(Santori)

In a small white church
overlooking the Aegean
there is a mural of Christ
when he was Greek.
Candles flicker in front
of it the way lights in the town
of Fira do at night. It's where
a wedding procession begins.
Two old men in black caps,
vests and thick mustaches
resting on their lips like fish
play violins as the bride
and groom in white with hair
as long as Greek flags follow,
family and friends trailing
behind them. They walk along
the caldera path, past ruins
that go back to the Minoans
but look like a man who just
lost another paycheck in
a card game. Locals come out
of their cliff homes to look down
yelling things you need your
dictionary to understand
along with smiles that are easy
to translate, until the last
person in the procession turns
around a bend and the music
fades into rock.

Like the Aegean

We are sitting on a beach
in Crete under an umbrella
that looks like a plate balanced
on a stick. My wife is in a string
bathing suit that I could tie
around my finger if I wanted
to remember everything I'm trying
to forget on this trip.

Two large topless women sit
near us speaking German,
their breasts the size of Berlin.
My wife says she likes sitting
near them since they make her
look skinny. I remind her she
already is and the only weight
she needs to lose is her family
who can't reach us here.

We notice four columns on a bluff
built in between Homer and Plato.
A cloud rests on them like a roof
making it a temple once again,
this time lasting long enough
for a short prayer or quick sacrifice.

A few yards away an older man
with a belly big as a globe
with lumps on it just north of Brazil
is telling a story to a friend
in English so broken his doctor
should place it in a sling until

it heals. We tune him out,
deciding we are going to stay here
as long as we can and grow ancient
but never old, like the Aegean
without a single wave in ruins.

Athens
(Plaka)

We stop at a taverna in Plaka
and pick a table outside where we
can have drinks and watch tourists.
The Acropolis rises up over the city
and in back of your wife's chair
who looks elegant wearing the Parthenon
as a crown. Ancient architects built
these narrow streets for citizens to walk,
horses, carts and maybe motor scooters
that to this day zigzag through the crowds.
Shop owners try to flatter then hustle
tourists into their shops. If anyone
looks German, Berlin is the best, if
Italian, long live the Pope and when
you walk by, the Bronx is beautiful.

At the table next to you a woman
speaks good English but sneezes in French.
At another, a Belgian couple is telling
jokes, getting drunk and laughing too loud.
When one comes over with his camera
and motions for you to take a picture,
it's a chance for you to get rid of them
with one shot. You take your time,
aim and shoot but miss by a mile.
As the tables fill around you everyone
is talking in a different language
and when they blend together it
becomes a language you can understand
and may learn to speak at home since
English hasn't been working as well
as it should lately.

At night you can't sleep
so you get out of bed,
and walk quietly on the hotel terrace
to see how Athens sleeps. Apartment
buildings are white boxes, their shades
closed, and won't open till dawn.
A motor scooter passes by on the street
below, sounding like a zipper being
pulled up on a pair of pants.
A block or two away a dog barks
with an accent but sounds
more like a hound than Greek.
A few moments later as you turn
to go inside, you glance at the moon
just to see another familiar face
from back home.

Parthenon

When you arrived in Athens
you discovered the Acropolis
was never named after a diner
down on Second Avenue and
the Parthenon could never fit in
your hand the way it always did
with coffee to go in a paper cup.
Your hotel was just blocks away.
At night you sat on the roof staring
at the ancient ruin, lights shining
on it—lit up like an old man
on good wine.

The next day you toured the Acropolis
so amazed you kept taking photos
of the Berilie gates, a few
columns, next the east cella, another
of a blonde in tight shorts. You pick
up a stone to put in your pocket
as a souvenir and to weigh you
down against the wind that kept
knocking your cap off like a bully
from the grammar school near Plaka.
Below the east pediment stronger
gusts blow dust off the ground
spinning it into a statue of Athena
who stares into your face until
another gust blows her away.

In the Acropolis museum
a young statue of a sixth century
boy holds onto a calf that is
draped over his shoulders like
a sweater. You admire him since

you were never able to hold onto
anything for that long in your life.
Near him is a maiden with the kind
of curves in her stone you couldn't help
noticing. Even with her hands missing
along with a bit of nose, she still
looks hot and hasn't put on an ounce
of marble around the hips for centuries.

Outside you stop to look down at Athens
that in the distance under the bright sun
looks like a path made of white pebbles
and beyond it the sea. You decide
to go for a swim and now
that you are convinced it takes more
than one god to run a universe,
you are able to jump up on a wall,
step down on rooftops and stroll
all the way to the Aegean.

III. The View from Here

Marriage Advice

The rain had stopped and the storm
that passed through left
the street wet, looking like mascara
running down a woman's face
who realizes this block isn't
just a one-night stand but an entire
neighborhood that can never
give her what she needs. And
with the front steps looking dry
enough to sit on, I went downstairs
to get some air.

The guy who lived in the apartment
above mine came out, said hello,
leaned against the railing, took out
a pack of cigarettes and offered me
one. I told him I quit as he lit up
inhaling so deeply the smoke went
past his lungs and straight to his toes.
I could tell he had another fight
with his wife. Living under them
for the past year, I knew marriage
sounded like thunder and broken glass.

He asked if I was married or ever
had been. I shook my head no,
so he decided to give me some advice,
then took another hit on his cigarette.
I didn't want any and didn't recognize
it coming out of his mouth
since it was covered in smoke
from his Marlboro.

Find yourself a Mormon; they're
not materialistic. Don't give a damn
about money, big cars, huge homes.
Just buy her a toaster and she'll
be impressed. And make sure
she's an orphan, then you won't have
to deal with her family. In-laws
become out-laws in a hurry.
Yup. If you got to get hitched,
an orphaned Mormon is the only
way to go.

As he talked I stared across
the street and noticed a small
piece of paper flutter like a butterfly
over a trashcan. In this part
of the city it's the first sign of spring.
When he finished up, I thanked
him for the advice and told him
I could go for that cigarette now.
Thought you quit he said.
I did, I told him. It's just that
I never stopped.

3:00 AM

The sound of Fred Astaire tap
dancing woke me. I looked over
at the clock, saw it was 3:00 am,
rubbed my eyes and realized
it was the sound of raindrops
hitting the tin roof of the cottage
we were renting in Key West.
I looked over at my wife still
sleeping, kissed her shoulder,
got out of bed and walked
out on the deck. I inhaled deeply;
even if I took this air, brought
it to the cleaners back home
and had it pressed and delivered
on a hanger, it would never
smell this clean.

Today was our first on the island
and I'm pleased we have two more
weeks, even happier to hear
temperatures in New York City
reached record lows and snow
down here only means poor reception
on a tv screen. We spent most
of the day on the beach at Fort Zach,
watched schooners sliding out
on the Gulf until they fit into bottles,
pelicans searching for only the wettest
waves, making it easy for them
to smash open and fly away with fish
in their beaks.

After dinner we stopped at a cigar
stand on Duval Street run by a Cuban

woman who spoke very little English
and since I speak just enough to get
by, I was able to buy a few hand-rolled
coronas. I go back inside to get one
come out on the deck again, sit on
a chair, lean back, light up and smoke
the moon.

The Cape

We stroll along the docks
watching fisherman carve
their catch, cut bellies fillet
and listen as they talk water.
We decide their skin is a leather
tourists will never buy.

On the pier we watch a ferry,
named after a storm that once
took homes under each wind
and carried them out to sea,
head toward a large white house
in the harbor that never tans.

We notice this is where
day ends, how heat breaks
the sun like an egg yolk, then lets
it melt over the horizon.
I point out it is the color
of your hair; you smile
take my hand, then tilt
your head, letting the sky
brush gently against my face.

Back home I put the lobsters
we bought on the kitchen floor
and joke them invaders.
You laugh, say it is a shame
they have to end this way
then load your camera and shoot.

We steam clams till
they grow tired and yawn,
then eat them with corn

we decide must have been
in love with soil to be this sweet.

We pile our empty shells
in a bowl next to the flowers
you picked and admire
how the walls bouquet
with their shadows.

The golden retriever from across
the road comes to our
screen door wagging its tail
at the tail of lobster meat
I dunk in butter. I tell him
to go away, then get up
to let him in, pat his head
and give him half.

Key West

Palm trees surrounding our cottage
applaud every breeze that passes through.
Small jets fly low into Key West Airport.
The next one that wakes me is the one
I'll climb up on the roof for, grab
then put it in the empty parrot cage
the owner keeps in the bedroom, train
it not to make so much noise, feed
it crackers since the airlines stopped
serving food, then send it on its way.

Unexpected cool weather came in
off the Gulf. I go across the street
from where we are renting to an old
conch shack that is being rebuilt. I
ask one of the workers who is putting
on a new coat of paint if he could
spare another since I didn't pack any
warm clothes. He looks into his bucket
and figures there is only enough left
over for a small sweater. I wear large—
thank him anyway.

Pregnant women in white dresses
are sails on a schooner leaving
the marina. It passes a cruise ship
that last night with all its lights on
could have been a high rise from Miami
which fell over on its side during
a storm last week and floated all
the way down here safely into port.
Tourists who poured out of it are walking
along Duvall with locals, college
kids and bikers who parade up
and down the street, revving their

engines because they can. All
walking and riding past crowded bars,
restaurants and small stands selling
cigars, just in case they need
another way to watch their money
burn and go up in smoke.

Chickens roam the streets—the rooster
next door whose timing is always
off keeps crowing dawn up at noon.
And the town claims ghosts of the many
writers who lived here like Hemingway,
Frost and Bishop can be seen walking
the streets at night. Perhaps that's why
it feels like home—all three have
been haunting me for years.

The sunsets here are so stunning
they fill Mallory Square with hundreds
of cameras tourists use to shoot
them. If you look close enough
you'll notice orange brush strokes—
makes me think the town council
must have a special effects department
to do repairs on color and clouds.

Each day ends for me on our porch,
gazing at a star right above
the tall palm trees that look
like Vegas showgirls backstage,
ready to go on when the lights
come up at dawn. It is there
every night, the size of a perfect
diamond no one can afford
and too distant to make a wish.
A star worth every bit of sky—
glittering.

My Mother's Clothes

My mother liked to wait
until after dinner and say
to my father that she couldn't
possibly attend some social event
that was coming up since
she had nothing at all to wear.
And my father liked to point out
that she had three large closets
filled with clothes; some outfits
she wore only once or never at
all. She also had enough shoes
for an army or whenever
the Marines needed to go off
to battle in pumps. She would
just stare into her cup filled
with tea the color of a good tan,
until he'd say go out tomorrow
and buy a new dress. Then he'd
reach into his pocket, try
not to smile and say his arm
was arthritic from years
of reaching back for his wallet
to give her clothes money.
And he was convinced after
reading in the paper that
Gimbels department store was
filing for Chapter 11 because
my mom stopped shopping
there six months earlier.

Three months after my father
died my mother bought her last
dress during a heat wave,
and in the middle of tumors

we didn't know were growing
in her stomach. This time
it was my sister who decided
my mother should wear that pink
outfit at her wake. When I
walked into the funeral home
and up to the casket, I
decided she looked great.
The color of the dress was vibrant,
alive and her hair was the color
of the gold coins I would have
paid to bring her back.
I started to think that maybe
she was just sleeping. So
rather than say a prayer I
leaned over and whispered
in her ear, Mom there's a
sale at Bloomingdale's tonight.
But rather than open her eyes,
jump up and say let's go you
drive, she just lay there.
She didn't move.

Exercise

At the far end of the fitness room
near the Nautilus three guys
argue sports until one coughs
up a basketball that rolls out
of his mouth and bounces on
the floor. They pick it up and go
into the gym to shoot hoops.
Even though there are free weights
I've learned everything has a price,
so I pass on them for now and get
on the Stair Master. After twenty
minutes even a corporate ladder
would be easier to climb and when
an elevator begins to make more
sense I get off, walk past
a woman on a stationary bike
reading a French travel magazine.
As she slowly pedals through
the streets of Paris I inspect
the weights, figuring it would be
smart to start with a dumbbell.
A big guy in the corner lying
on his back on a bench grunts
under a barbell, on each end
weights the size of truck tires
remind me that in a half hour
I'll be able to roll out of here.
I then get on the treadmill, start
a slow jog and notice the guy
running next to me has his shirt off,
showing off his six pack that looks
nothing like the Amstels waiting
for me in the refrigerator
when I get home. And at some

point during the first quarter mile
I feel refreshed, turn up the speed,
my heart beginning to pound
as if it were falling in love with sweat,
and when my legs begin to blur,
I know no one, absolutely no one
in that room can catch me.

White Curtain

The past seven days
have been mild—
temperatures in the sixties
and low seventies made it
feel like a week of hippies.

Today it's snowing heavy,
a white curtain with April
behind it. The Weather Channel
calls the storm unusual
for this time of year. The radio
says it's strange, a freak—
another Janet Slotski who did
the first string of the JV
football team after our high school
pep rally. She claimed she just
wanted to help us through
another losing season.

I've been wanting to get out
of the city and take a trip
since I can no longer afford
traveling back to my childhood,
perhaps to the Mediterranean
but the closest I get to Athens
is the diner around the block
that fries everything in grease.

A woman in the apartment
directly across from mine
walks around her bedroom
with the blinds up, lights on
and her clothes off. I want
to invite her over then decide
to let her prance around like that
instead to help melt the snow.

She is just another reminder
that I need to be alone for awhile.
To keep proving it to myself,
when I hear the phone I wait
for the last ring before picking
it up to make sure no one
is there every time.

Boys Can't be Trusted

The My niece likes to sit on my lap
every time I visit. When she wants
me to make up a story rather than read
it from a book, she'll say read me a story
from your mouth. I've been quite prolific
with titles like: *The Fir Tree That Wore Imitation
Fur*, *The Turtle Who Made Calls on His Shell
Phone* and *The Poet Trees in the Forest*.
My niece likes to hear about boys who get
in trouble, since girls are smarter and nicer.
I decided then to add some disguised
autobiographical sketches. Two favorites
from the Boy Series are: *The Dumb Boy
in Math Class* and *The Boy Who Could Balance
a Basketball on His Finger but Couldn't
Balance His Checkbook*. So I was surprised
when she told me about the boys in her
pre-school class. Michael Chicatelli is very
smart and knows everything about dinosaurs.
Paulie Floater has been showing her tricks
on his yo-yo that only he can do and Walt
Wheeler's father is Walt Disney. How could I
tell her this is how it starts, these little creeps
can't even spell their names but already have
lines to get over on a pretty girl. Next they'll
be ringing her door dressed in expensive clothes,
their European sports cars with names no one
can pronounce sparkling in her driveway, and
jewelry they'll want to give her, then kiss
across her neck. I couldn't let these boys get
away with this and later would have to talk to
her father. But until then and since my niece

was still curled on my lap, I began a new story called: *Why Boys Who Like Dinosaurs, Yo-Yo Tricks and Say Their Fathers are Famous are Liars and Can't Be Trusted.*

Scattered Crumbs

You stop in a café and order
a coffee from a woman a little
bigger than the scones on sale
next to the muffins with icing
the color of snow piled so high
they could close a school. You take
the empty table near the window
with a half empty cup of cocoa
and scattered crumbs looking
the way Santa might leave it
after a snack on Christmas Eve.

You look out, take a sip then sit
still in order to watch the city move.
A bus rattles like dentures in the cold
on its way cross town; a flock
of pigeons near the curb walk on feet
shaped like pitch forks, their heads
moving back and forth—pistons
to an engine even a mechanic could never
fix. A young boy passing them holds
on to his mother's hand and onto
a string tied to a balloon. When it breaks
free he watches it until it is as high
as Chet Baker's voice and begins to cry.
An old woman crossing the street
alone gets angry, begins to yell,
makes a few important points and
by the time she reaches the opposite
corner, wins the argument and smiles.
It's impressive, you think, how quickly
she settled things.

On a whim you get up and head
into the church next door. You could
have sworn it was Catholic
but the saints near the altar look
Lutheran in the shadows and the rest
aren't even Christian, they're marble.
You find candles flickering near the last
pew, place money in the donation
box then find one that doesn't burn
on both ends, light it and pray it doesn't
burn the bottom of an angel's foot
on the wall a few inches above it.

After you get home you start
washing the dishes, then reach for
the towel that looks like the small
Yorkie a woman down the block
walks every day. When it begins
to growl as you dry the first glass,
you decide to finish later, turn off
the faucet, put on your coat, then
pick up the towel again and take
it out for a long walk.

Donuts

I told you I look
like that movie star
who was on the cover
of *Time* last week or at least
resemble him the way
Chicago does New York if
you stand on a street corner
then look sideways.
And the blood flowing
through my veins has never
been blue—the closest I ever
get to royalty is when I play
my Duke Ellington CDs.
At least he taught me how
to swing when I gave up
walking. I also learned
when I was down South
that the Bible Belt could never
hold up my pants no matter
how tight I buckled it and
that everything is connected.
A rooster I saw moving back
and forth in front of a barn
looked like Mick Jagger strutting
back and forth on stage at a Stones
concert in Atlanta. It's the same
reason smoke rings are donuts
without the carbs and why
you should grab love wherever
you find it, even if it costs
a couple of bucks and comes
with all the coffee you can drink
and a side of fries.

The Cat That Could Fly

The cat we had as kids never
ate the food we gave him.
Instead he hunted the backyard,
grew heavy on sparrow and robins.
When he spotted small birds he'd freeze,
even in August, turn concrete, stone
twitched more, then he'd pounce,
his jaws filled with thrashing wings
as if his mouth was trying to fly
away from his head. The day
he killed a squirrel and left the body
like a dead Cossack at our back
doorstep, our mother's scream
made trees rustle.

At night in winter we heard him
fight other cats; in summer
it was the sound of car tires spinning
on ice. The gash in his forehead never
healed, his ears were shaped like figs.

The day my brothers and I found him
on the side of the road where he was hit
by a car or a truck, we covered him
with leaves and sticks, his eye staring
like the dime at the bottom of my pocket.
When our four-year-old sister asked
why he didn't come home anymore
we told her he ate so many birds
he just flew away. For months
every time she went out to play, she'd
first stop by the door, shield her eyes
with her hands and look up at the sky.

Anniversary

It has been a year today
as family and friends
form a small circle with heads
bowed, the minister asking
each of us to say a few words
about Ben. The first woman,
her eyes floating in water,
and no bigger than a cough
is comforted just knowing
he is no longer in pain.
The man standing next to her
with hair the color of smoke
says almost the same thing
and adds on heaven. When
it is my turn I say the Yankees
got A Rod and as of today
they are seven games in front
of Boston. I figured someone
should tell him since he was
a sports fanatic. I didn't mention
his favorite team, The Eagles,
choked in the playoffs. He
might have known this already
since bad news travels fast
no matter where you are.
I almost added how mad
I was at him for not taking
his meds, and when he took
his own life, he also took
a part of ours especially
his sister's, my wife of only a year
holding onto my hand, trembling.
And when the last person
in the circle offers up another

prayer, I'm thinking about
how I've watched night, temperatures,
even stocks fall and knew
I could do nothing to stop them.
Then I picture him on the bridge
ready to jump. I'm running
towards him again, pleading for him
to wait, yelling at the voices
in his head to shut up.
I would have done anything
to have been there,
to stop him from falling—
anything or at the very least
died trying.

Sunset in the Refrigerator

The man who sells fruit
from a stand on the corner
of York and Sixty-Eighth has
a name you can't pronounce
and is so long that if you stood it
up on its last letter it would be
several inches taller than he is.
Today he has grapefruit the size
of softballs the kind your mom used to
pitch to anyone starting a diet;
apples perfect for teachers desks,
and watermelon cut into boats
with passengers of pits and dark
blueberries filling small green
baskets like periods the school
up the street is using to stop sentences.

He grabs a Crenshaw melon, takes
out his pocket knife and cuts
into it pulling out a slice that sits
like a smile in his hand. You agree
how ripe it is as he cuts a bigger
grin out of a cantaloupe and says
it's the color of the sun then gives you
a piece to sample. It is sweet,
tastes like the sky and is the color
of the sun when it warms your back
and makes you turn to watch it melt
over the high rises and melt down
over their sides on Seventy-second Street.
He then sells you the best melon
he can find and in a few minutes
you will be home relaxing, waiting
for your wife to return as the sun sets
next to a bottle of wine
in your refrigerator.

The Reincarnation of Bagels

The smell of coffee coming out
of diners makes sure the sun
is up and bagels are a way to get
things rolling. A few trucks and cabs
hit potholes and rattle you the way
losing jobs once did. Girls walk by
in shorts so tight you can hardly breathe.
A cat stares down from a fire escape
his eyes the size of dimes – all he can look
at for twenty cents. The entire sidewalk
is taken over by a woman walking
in the middle of ten dogs. She is holding
on to an octopus of leashes and moves
as if she is in a pond up to her knees
in fur. An old man in clothes that fit
him like an unmade bed with a cup
in his hand for anyone's change, watches
as they go by.

Body bags of garbage are piled up
in front of buildings by maintenance men.
Some polish gold posts so bright
they capture reflections, stretching your
face down onto the sidewalk where
you almost trip over your chin
The cool sound of air conditioners
are a reminder to buy a new one
today. Yours broke down but you
are more fortunate than most and were
able to play your Stan Getz CDs –
his sax cooled off the entire apartment.

A baker who has been working
since dawn stands outside his shop
on a break, places a cigarette in his mouth,
lights it then blows smoke rings
he sometimes dips in icing and places
in the window next to the cakes then makes
them the day's special. On the next block,
a painter is scraping the wall of a law firm.
His white overalls and t-shirt are splattered
with different colored paints, looking as if
he dressed today in a Pollack canvas.
Across the street they have begun to knock
down St. John's Church the Cardinal closed
to save money. A Foot Locker will go up
in its place – most of the parish won't travel
to the church across town and are planning
to convert to Nike. The lead article in the
newspaper reports Christ left over the weekend
then took a subway downtown to look
for work since there were no jobs or was over-
qualified for an opening in a Catholic church.
He told a reporter he will explore some smaller
churches below Fourteenth Street even Lutheran
or Methodist. It really doesn't matter.

Lucky Man

On the corner of Second Avenue
waiting for the light to turn
red, my legs begin to vibrate
then my hands. I almost run
to the ER three blocks away
until I realize I've been standing
over the subway and the No. 4
on its way uptown. I calm down
and relax knowing by the time
it reaches Fourteenth Street I'll be cured.
When the light turns, I wait
a few moments since I hate
change, adjust to the new color,
then hurry across the street.

A new deli has signs stuck on
its windows advertising soda,
beer and heroes. I don't need
drinks and I doubt if Michael Jordan
is in stock, who would be worth
the $4.50 to help me with my jump
shot. I lean against a meter to decide
where to go then put a quarter
in it when a cop walks by
to prove I'm not loitering now
that I parked. It turns out
I am thirsty; even with ten
minutes left on the meter, I head
for the bar at the end of the block.

As soon as I take a seat
my mind finally cracks but I don't
panic and when it happens
again, I'm relieved it's only

a pool game in the back room.
I'm proud that I didn't panic
or lose my head this time.
To celebrate I make sure all
the beers I order lose theirs.

On my way home, I pass
the tenement near Third, the tall
one with at least six stories,
the top three I never even read.
Sitting on the steps a guy
thinner than my wallet, asks
if I want pussy. It reminds me
of the two kittens a woman
on the first floor gave me, that are now
sleeping in a box in the kitchen.
When he asks again, I tell him
no thanks I have all I can handle
at home. As I cross the street
he yells, then you are a lucky
man. A couple of seconds later
it dawns on me, the sun moving
from my shoes to my eyes,
that he's right. I am a lucky man,
a very lucky man.

Afterlife

My parents were right about
an afterlife. Even though they died
six years ago, I talk to them every day.
Tonight they are in the living room
while I'm in bed with a woman
I met in a bar. They are waiting
patiently for me—my mom is ironing
the pants I flung on the couch,
making sure the creases are sharp
enough to cut the apple pies she made
me as a kid. My dad sits
with the newspaper in his favorite
chair I took from their house after it
was sold. He likes to open to the obituaries
these days, relieved that he's not
in them anymore.

The woman I'm sweating over
was the hottest thing I ever saw just a few
drinks ago and still is as long as I keep
my eyes closed. Her legs keep slapping
against my thighs, so I stay on top of her,
afraid if I get off she'll begin to fly
and bang her head against a wall.
If I knew her name I'd use it, tell her
things like it's almost time to stop; in
a couple of minutes we give up instead.
Neither of us could come and when
it is clear she isn't going to go, I ask
her to.

She gets up, searches for her clothes
scattered around the floor as if they exploded.
The sweat on her body could be grease

the way she slides into things, then looks
in the mirror to fluff her hair with her fingertips.
No matter how hard she tries it still
hangs like curtains I've been meaning
to buy for the window. I don't even try
to explain why I need her to leave,
that my parents could never be in
the next room after the way cancer ate,
or how I have so much to discuss
with them, now that I found out what
it really means to be dead.

The View from Here

I walk east along 72nd Street
to where it ends and overlooks
the FDR Drive that runs next
to the waves jogging on the East River.
I sit on one of the new wooden
benches that after a year is already
the color of pigeons. I put on a few
pounds but the traffic on the Drive
is still heavier and I would feel
closer to Queens if Roosevelt Island
didn't come between us. Its three
tall smokestacks look like anti-
aircraft guns pointed at sky, in case
terrorists try again. And today
the sky is clear except for a cloud
shaped like a pillow that makes
the Macy's white sale look
dull. I can make out a jet that
is heading for one of the airports
and is small enough to fit in the belly
of a gull standing on a barge.
And when my wife finally arrives
she walks towards me holding
her hands in front of her with all
fingers moving up and down
as if floating on water so I can
inspect her new nail polish. I tell
her it's the color of the tug
built like a bulldog now under
the 59th Street Bridge. She smiles, sits
down next to me, holds onto my
right arm, looks out over the river
and sighs, then helps me the way she always
does, quietly letting her eyes fill with
everything I couldn't possibly fit
into mine.

Kevin Pilkington is a member of the writing faculty at Sarah Lawrence College and teaches a workshop in the graduate department at Manhattanville College. He is the author of six collections: his collection **Spare Change** was the La Jolla Poets Press National Book Award winner and his chapbook won the Ledge Poetry Prize. His collection entitled **Ready to Eat the Sky** was published by River City Publishing as part of their new poetry series and was a finalist for an Independent Publishers Books Award. His collection entitled **In the Eyes of a Dog** was published by New York Quarterly Books. His poetry has appeared in many anthologies including *Birthday Poems: A Celebration*, *Western Wind*, and *Contemporary Poetry of New England*. Over the years, he has been nominated for four Pushcarts and has appeared in *Verse Daily*. His poems and reviews have appeared in numerous magazines including: *Poetry, Ploughshares, Iowa Review, Boston Review, Yankee, Hayden's Ferry, Columbia, North American Review*, etc. A novel entitled **Summer Shares** is forthcoming from ArcheBooks.

Acknowledgement is made to the following periodicals in which these poems have appeared in various forms:

The Adroit Journal......*The Distance Between Fog and Times Square*
Columbia: A Journal of Literature and Art......*Santorini*
Confrontation......*Looking for Work*
Crying Sky......*Donuts, The View from Here, The Week the Factory and Pancreas Closed Down*
Green Mountains Review......*Travel*
Inkwell......*Key West, Greek Wedding*
Jelly Bucket......*Milk, Walking Across America, The Cat That Could Fly*
Light Millennium......*Scattered Crumbs*
Lumina......*On Cold Days Like This, Donuts*
New York Quarterly......*White Curtain*
The North American Review......*The Unemployed Man Who Became A Tree*
Permafrost......*On the Corner*
Rattle......*St. Andrew's Head*
The Tampa Review......*Insomnia*
The Texas Review......*Afterlife*
Valparaiso Review......*Capri, Parthenon, Promises, Sunset in the Refrigerator*
Vermont Literary Review......*Camden*
The Westchester Review......*Anniversary, Boys Can't Be Trusted*

Some of the poems have appeared in the following chapbooks:

Reading Stone, Jeanne DuVal Editions
St. Andrew's Head, Camber Press